CAROLYN MILLER

ABOUT THE SERIES

The Composer's Choice series showcases piano works by an exclusive group of composers. Each collection contains classic piano pieces that were carefully chosen by the composer, as well as brand-new pieces written especially for the series. Helpful performance notes are also included.

ISBN 978-1-4803-4100-5

WILLIS MUSIC

EXCLUSIVELY DISTRIBUTED BY

HAL•LEONARD®
CORPORATION

7777 W. BLUEMOUND RD. P.O. BOX 13819 MILWAUKEE, WI 53213

Visit Hal Leonard Online at
www.halleonard.com

FROM THE COMPOSER

I hope you enjoy discovering the many patterns that help with the learning and memorization of the pieces in this book. You will find a wide variety of styles and tempos, and I think you will soon realize that the pieces *sound* more difficult than they are to play. It is my hope that you will enjoy playing these solos and have a lifelong love of music!

Carolyn Miller

CONTENTS

ROLLING RIVER

"Rolling River" is one of my favorite pieces – it sounds pretty, and yet is not hard to play. I love to hear it played in a flowing style, with relaxed hands and correct pedaling. Students should be made aware of the simple chord structure and the ABA form. I was thrilled and excited when this piece was performed by Regis Philbin on national television back in 1992!

PING PONG

Have you ever played ping pong? If so, you will be able to relate to this piece! Keep the staccatos as light as possible. Grace notes may be a new adventure for some, but once you master them, they are really fun to play. The Coda is a group of patterned notes in different octaves. Make sure to master the last measure, especially because there is no *ritard* at the end.

MARCH OF THE GNOMES

"March of the Gnomes" is a descriptive march that requires a very steady beat. The left hand (LH) should be relaxed in order to create a perfect, bouncing staccato. The right hand (RH) should also be relaxed so as to create solid double-notes (3rds). Be sure to notice the repetitions in various octaves.

MORNING DEW

Aim for a singing melody and a graceful motion. Pay special attention to the sequences in the A section. Learning the chords in the B section before putting your hands together would also be very beneficial. Think of beautiful, peaceful thoughts.

RAZZ-A-MA-TAZZ

This is a lively and spirited piece! Knowing and understanding the cadence chords in F Major before playing this solo will make learning it much easier. Be aware of the similar patterns that are to be played in different octaves.

THE PIPER'S DANCE

This is a lively dance and must have a good, steady rhythmic flow. Try to feel it "in 2" instead of "in 6." The B section moves to E Minor (the relative minor); note the pattern and the B Major chord. Also, make sure to practice the long G Major arpeggio in the last two measures.

THE GOLDFISH POOL

When I play this piece, I think of a gentle swirling in the water. Keep the fingers close to the keys and just let it flow. The B section sequence represents a little waterfall in the pool. Here's a practice suggestion: repeat each pattern 3 times with the RH, 3 times with the LH, and then with the cross-hand pattern.

MORE FIREFLIES

This solo is a lot like the original "Fireflies" (HL00405627)–it has a similar triplet pattern and long arpeggios. Learning the LH cadence chords in G Minor and then naming the arpeggiated chords will assist in learning (and memorizing). Work especially hard to keep the fireflies on the last line flying into the horizon!

Rolling River

Carolyn Miller

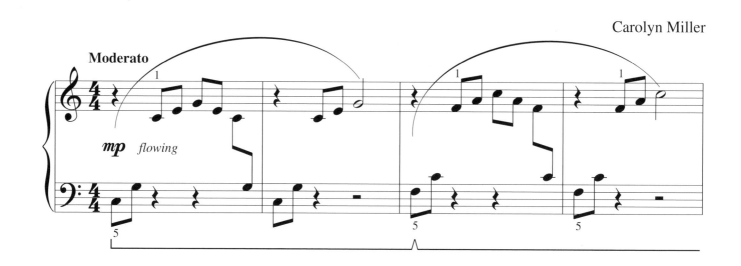

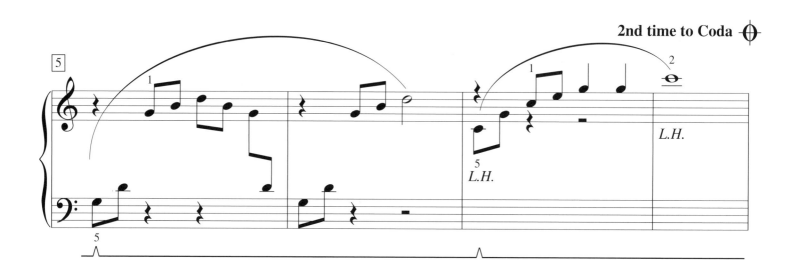

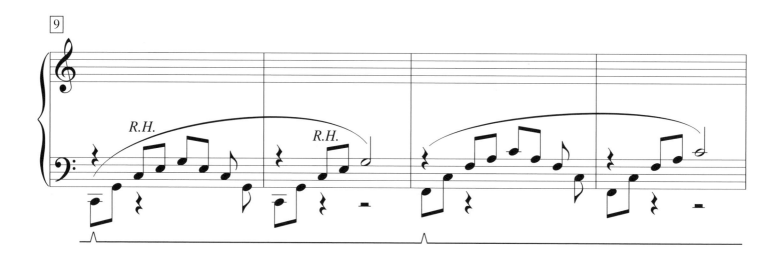

Ping Pong

Carolyn Miller

Allegro moderato

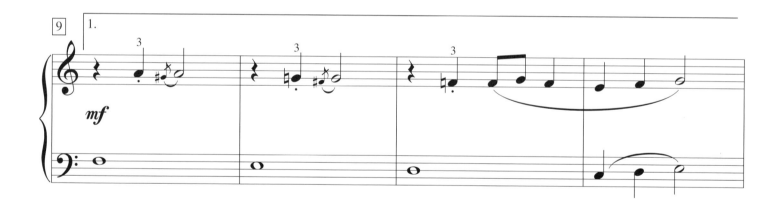

March of the Gnomes

Carolyn Miller

Morning Dew

Andante cantabile

Carolyn Miller

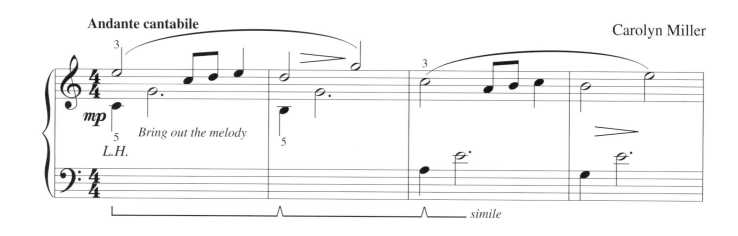

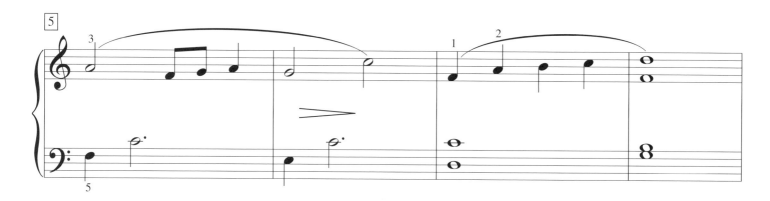

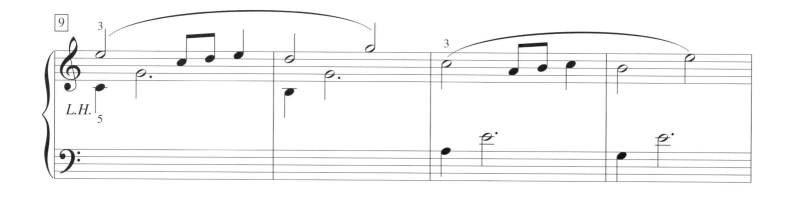

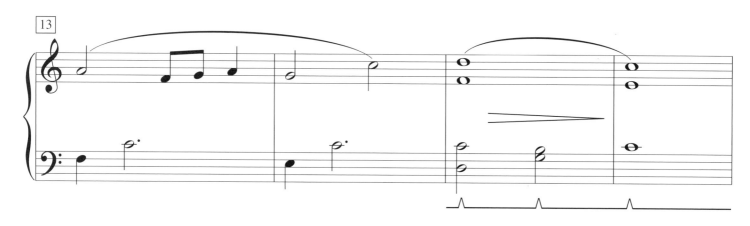

Razz-A-Ma-Tazz

Carolyn Miller

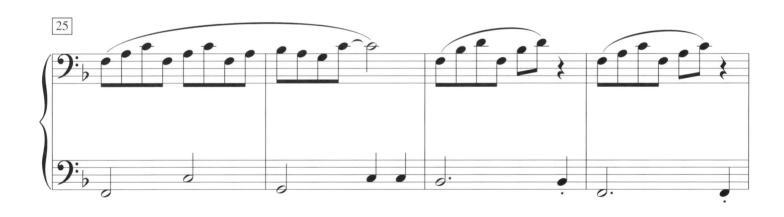

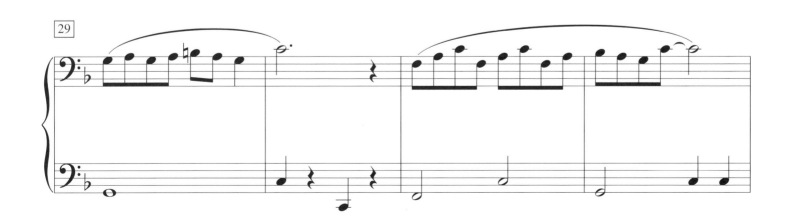

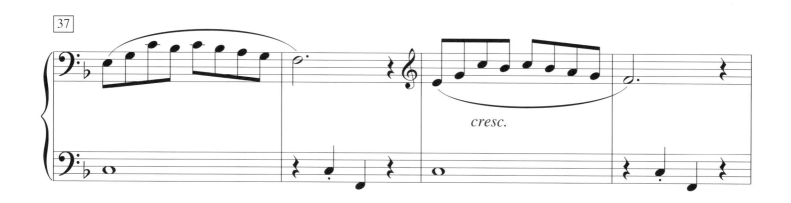

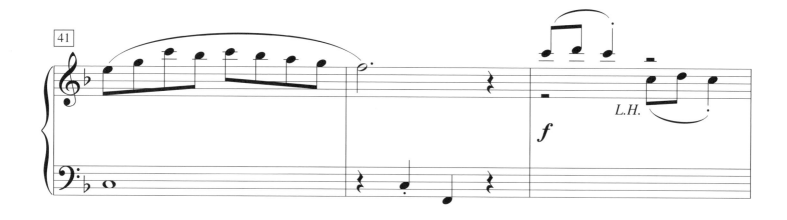

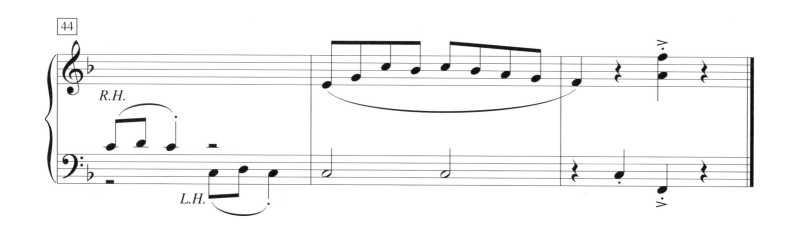

The Piper's Dance
(Gigue)

Carolyn Miller

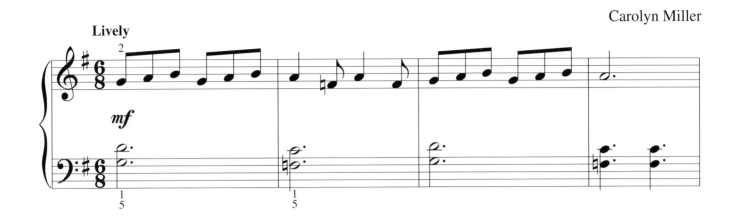

The Goldfish Pool

Carolyn Miller

(goldfish swim elegantly)

More Fireflies

Carolyn Miller

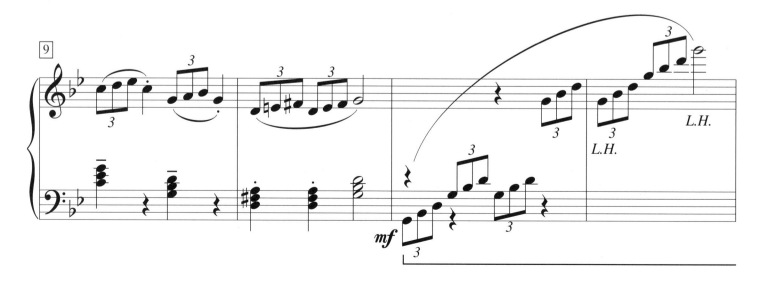

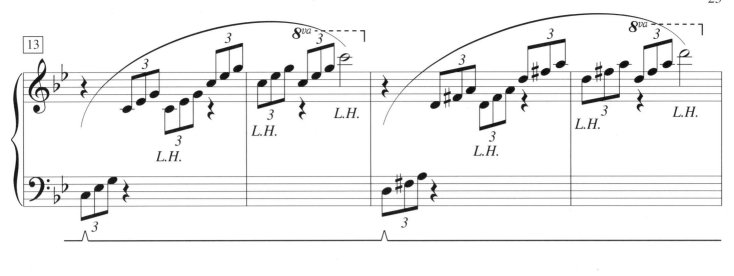

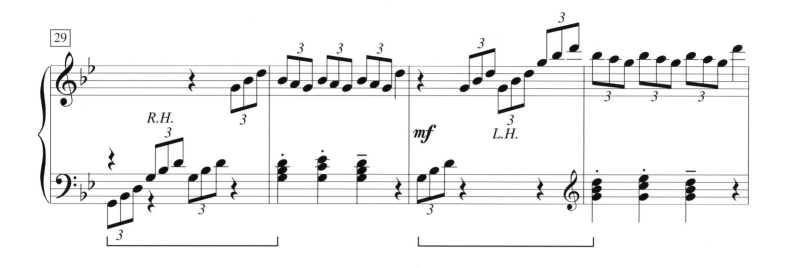

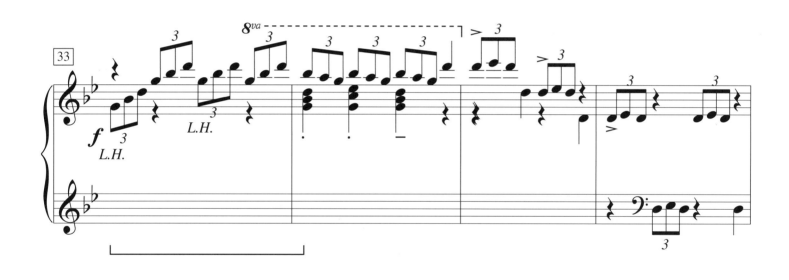